No Offense

Communication
Guaranteed Not to Offend

Karl W. Beckstrand

Premio Publishing & Gozo Books
Midvale, UT, USA
PremioBooks.com

No Offense: Communication Guaranteed Not to Offend

Karl Beckstrand

Premio Publishing & Gozo Books © 2013
Midvale, UT, USA
ebook ISBN: 978-1301370962
ISBN: 978-0615876863

PREMIO
PUBLISHING

CONTENTS

No Offense

Karl Beckstrand

No Offense

No Offense

No Offense

No Offense

No Offense

No Offense

No Offense

No Offense

No Offense

No Offense

No Offense

No Offense

No Offense

No Offense

No Offense

Karl Beckstrand

No Offense

No Offense

No Offense

No Offense

No Offense

No Offense

THE END

Karl Beckstrand

About the Author

College media instructor **Karl Beckstrand** is the award-winning and best-selling author/illustrator of 27 multicultural titles and more than 60 e-books. His western thriller, To Swallow the Earth, won a 2016 International Book Award, and his multicultural kids' books have been lauded by *Publisher's Weekly*, Kirkus, *The Horn Book*, and *School Library Journal.* He has lived abroad and worked with people from all continents (except Antarctica). His work reflects cultural diversity—not only in protagonists, but in collaborators (his illustrators hail from Latin America, Europe, and Asia).

Mr. Beckstrand earned a B.A. in journalism from Brigham Young University, an M.A. in international relations and conflict resolution from American Public University, and a certificate from Film A. Academy. He interned for a publisher in Massachusetts and for Congress in D.C. Formerly a technical recruiter in Silicon Valley, Beckstrand's early work was produced by small publishers. Since 2004 he has run Premio Publishing & Gozo Books.

Beckstrand contrasts traditional with digital publishing as a regular contributor in print, television, radio, podcasts, stage, and screen. He's been an in-flight Spanish-English interpreter for Angel Flight (medical nonprofit), a volunteer chaplain at Stanford University Hospital, and was a founding member of the San Francisco-based LGBTQIA group, The Freemen.

His Y.A. fiction, self-help, short stories, Spanish & bilingual books, mysteries, STEM, and nonfiction/biographies feature characters of color and usually end with a twist. He has sung in a couple of rock bands, can build a pc, water and snow ski, kayak, handle a bow and arrow, volleyball, firearms, and horses (typically not at the same time).

Beckstrand has presented to Taiwan's Global Leadership for Youth, city and state governments, festivals, and schools. His work has appeared in: Amazon, Baker & Taylor, Barnes & Noble, Costco, Deseret Book, Follett, Apple/iBooks, Ingram, Target & Walmart (online), and **PremioBooks.com**.

MORE
FUN

Libros online books FREE/GRATIS: PremioBooks.com

Other titles by Karl Beckstrand:

The Bridge of the Golden Wood: A Parable on How to Earn a Living
God Adores You: Beyond Either/Or Thinking to Your Most Fulfilling LGBTQIA Life
Horse & Dog Adventures in Early California: Short Stories & Poems
Ma MacDonald Flees the Farm: It's not a pretty picture ... book
She Doesn't Want the Worms! – ¡Ella no quiere los gusanos!
Crumbs on the Stairs – Migas en las escaleras: A Mystery
Sounds in the House – Sonidos en la casa: A Mystery
Samuel Sailing: The True Story of an Immigrant Boy
Agnes's Rescue: The True Story of an Immigrant Girl
It Came from under the High Chair: A Mystery
It Ain't Flat: A Memorizable Book of Countries
The Dancing Flamingos of Lake Chimichanga
GROW: How We Get Food from Our Garden
Bright Star, Night Star: An Astronomy Story
Polar Bear Bowler: A Story Without Words
Arriba Up, Abajo Down at the Boardwalk
Bad Bananas: A Story Cookbook for Kids
Butterfly Blink: A Book Without Words
Great Cape o' Colors - Capa de colores
Gopher Golf: A Wordless Picture Book
Why Juan Can't Sleep: A Mystery?
Muffy & Valor: A True Story
To Swallow the Earth
Anna's Prayer
Ida's Witness

If you like our stories, please comment online.

www.ingramcontent.com/pod-product-compliance
Lightning Source LLC
Chambersburg PA
CBHW060050050426
42448CB00011B/2391